Business Planning
For
Real Estate Agents

A Step-By-Step Guide For
Creating An Effective Business Plan

by

Matt Williams

For additional content and information on how to obtain the spreadsheets found in Appendix A and Appendix B, please visit www.BusinessPlanningForRealEstateAgents.com

"We each build our own future.
We are the architects of our own
fortune."

- Appius Claudius Caecus
(340 BC - 270 BC)

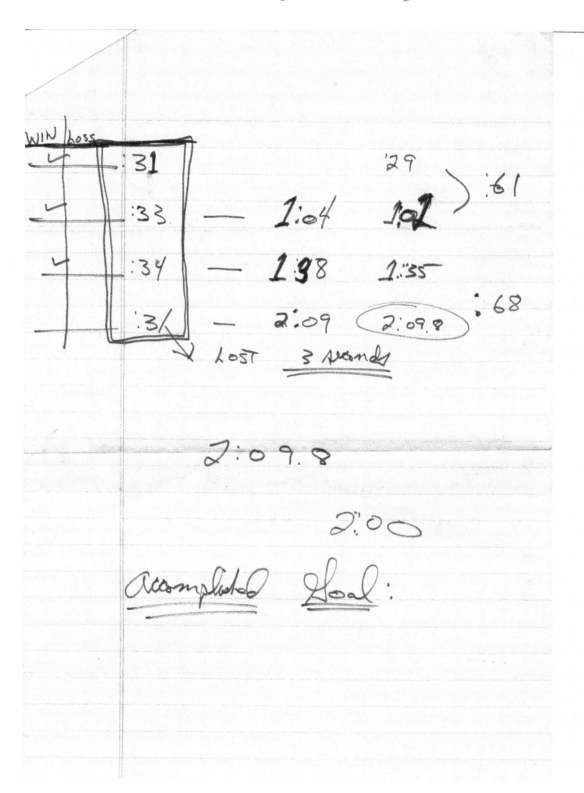

WIN / LOSS

:31

:33 — 1:04   '29 1:02 } :61

:34 — 1:98 1:35

:31 — 2:09 (2:09.8) :68

LOST 3 seconds

2:09.8

2:00

Accomplished Goal :

Dedication

To my brother Scott, my first mentor and the person who introduced me to the concept of planning when I was 14 years old and the most important thing in my life was to run a half-mile in under 2 minutes and 10 seconds.

Business Planning For Real Estate Agents

Contents

Preface

Some time ago I wrote a book for real estate agents about how to create a winning business plan entitled, *Planning for Success in Real Estate Sales – Your Guide to Creating a Winning Business Plan.* It is not a very large book – just 60 double-spaced pages. It can be read in less than an hour.

The book has sold well and I was pleased with the comments I received from those who employed the principles the book taught. But the book was largely conceptual. I explained primarily the 'why' of business planning and not as much the 'how'. My purpose was not to get too deep 'into the weeds' of numerical details, analyzing past performance, devising detailed budgets and such. I did cover that, but it was secondary to a general explanation of why an agent should have a business plan.

This book is different. It does go into the weeds. It is mostly analytical and only a little conceptual. This is a workbook. It is meant to be written in. It should be worn in by the time you have developed your plan and worn out by the end of the year. It was not written to replace *Planning for Success in Real Estate Sales,* it was written to complement it. If you follow this workbook step by step, you will create for your use a detailed, personalized business plan. The first book tells <u>why</u> you want to have a plan and the back story for the three components – goals, systems, and a means for staying on track. This book is more hands on. If you already have my first book, this book will still be useful. If you have this book and want a deeper understanding of the reasons for a business plan, reading *Planning for Success in Real Estate Sales* will be time well spent.

———————

I struggled through many of my early years as a real estate agent, my income rising and falling with market conditions. It was not until I was introduced to the concept of business planning that I learned that my level of production was not a matter of fate and dependent on outside forces. I was the one who determined what my income would be, not the market. I just had to give careful consideration to what I wanted to accomplish and how I was going to accomplish it.

On my own I created a business plan and soon experienced firsthand just how effective such a plan can be. Later, as a manager for one of the nation's largest real estate companies, I taught some of the more ambitious agents how to use a business plan. When I opened my own company in 2002, business planning was part of our corporate culture.

> *Agents that create and then follow an effective plan list more houses, sell more houses, make more money, and do so with less stress and less waste of time, effort and money.*

Agents that create and then follow an effective business plan list more houses, sell more houses, make more money, and do so with less stress and less waste of time, effort and money. It's a fact. Unfortunately, many agents have never been introduced to the concept of business planning. Of those who at least have heard of the benefits of business planning, most do not have anyone to teach them what to do.

And sadly, when some companies do conduct 'business planning sessions', they do a poor job.

I recall the 'business planning sessions' we managers had with our agents when I worked for that large national company. We would sit with the agent with a spreadsheet in front of us and ask, "How many houses are you going to sell next year?" They would tell us a number and we would write the answer in the appropriate box on the company-provided form. Then we'd ask, "How many listings are you going to take?" They would tell us that number and we would write that number in a different box. We'd then take their answers, divide them by 12 and presto, we had the monthly 'goals'. The whole process took about 10 minutes. There was no discussion of how they would achieve these numbers. We'd file the plan in their folder where it would never be seen again. The agent would leave the office, relieved the ordeal was over, and then go back to doing business as they always had done it.

This is not business planning.

Actually it is, but it is poor planning. In fact, not having any plan at all is a business plan. It is a plan whose foundation is taking whatever business happens to come your way. It is a plan, but not a good one.

I encourage you to develop an effective plan, put it into action, and see how your business, income, and life's choices grow. Once you experience the many benefits the plan and the planning process provide, you will never want to work without one.

Introduction

When people want a venture to be successful they create a plan that will result in the desired outcome.

When a builder builds a house he doesn't just dig a hole and start haphazardly nailing pieces of lumber together. Instead he follows the architect's blueprint. That blueprint (the plan) essentially is a roadmap that directs the builder and ensures the house is built properly and efficiently.

A mechanic working on a car will follow a systematic plan to diagnose trouble and then another plan to fix the problem. A father assembling a bicycle for his daughter on Christmas Eve will use the instruction manual (a plan) to be sure the job is done right and in time for a Christmas morning surprise. A chef will follow the recipe (a plan) to ensure he has all the ingredients and they are added in the right order so his creation is pleasing to the person who ordered it.

Plans are an essential element of successful outcomes and a detailed business plan is essential for real estate agents. The overwhelming majority of real estate agents earn far less than they are capable of, in part, because they don't work from a plan. From day-to-day they simply don't do the things they should be doing. Because of the nature of the real estate sales business, not having a plan as a real estate agent is particularly damaging. Here's why:

One of the more attractive aspects of a career in real estate sales is the freedom the job affords. Most agents work as independent contractors and as such are free to go to and fro without the kind of oversight an employee working on an assembly line, at a school cafeteria or in an office job would have. A real estate agent can literally do any activity she wants every day. For example, she can spend her time previewing houses, prospecting for clients, gossiping in the office, driving buyers around, or any one of dozens of things . . . including doing nothing at all.

The problem is not every activity results in success. In fact, most of the activities result in, if not failure, then at least underproduction and underutilization of the agent's ability and resources.

This is one of the reasons why so many agents fail at real estate and why most agents perform at just a fraction of their potential. They just don't do the right things consistently. That's why they need a business plan.

Think of a business plan as a roadmap. It lays out before you the path you should follow to reach the destination you desire.

Just as the blueprint shows the builder what he is to do, the real estate agent's business plan shows her what she needs to do. By showing her what she is to do, her focus is directed away from the things she should not do. Agents without plans tend to fall victim to the 'prettiest butterfly' syndrome – chasing after the prettiest butterfly that flitters into their life. In doing so they are often led astray. Rather than investing three productive hours prospecting for listings, the real estate agent drops what she is doing and instead spends her time searching for houses for an $800,000 buyer that called when she was on floor time. A business plan guards against that kind of behavior and outcome.

Think of a business plan as a roadmap. It lays out before you the path you should follow to reach the destination you desire. A good plan will have checkpoints along the way so you can ensure that you are on track. The more specific you can make that plan, the more likely you will remain on it and the more likely you will reach your destination.

In this pages that follow, I will help you develop a specific, personalized business plan that, if you follow it, will significantly improve your chances of achieving your goals.

The Basic Components of a Business Plan

There are three fundamental parts to a real estate agent's business plan – goals, systems, and a means for staying on track.

Goals are simply what you want to accomplish. As a real estate agent you will have many goals. Specific numbers for income, transaction sides[1], listings, buyer sides, etc. are examples of goals. To be effective, goals must be specific, measurable, and meaningful to you. You cannot begin a journey unless you know where you want to go. Goals, and particularly your primary goal, are your destination and the first thing you need to establish in creating your business plan. In Part 1 I'll show you how to set goals.

> *The most important thing a real estate agent does is establish new relationships with people who are interested in buying and selling real estate.*

Once you have determined <u>what</u> you want to accomplish, the next step is to determine <u>how</u> you will accomplish it. To do this we utilize "systems". A system is simply a series of actions performed in order to achieve a particular outcome. If we are looking to initiate relationships with homeowners, we may use systems that involve contacting FSBOs and owners of homes that were on the market but did not sell (Expireds), Direct Mail including Just Listed or Just Sold cards, letters to out of area owners, letters to long-time owners, or just postcards offering a free market analysis. Other systems include hosting open houses or informational seminars, attending consumer expos, or doing anything else that will put you in front of buyers and sellers. The most important thing a real estate agent does is establish new relationships with people interested in buying and selling real estate. There are many ways to develop new relationships – some more effective than others – but each can be formulated into a system.

For example, an agent may have a Direct Mail (DM) system. The agent has determined that over the course of the next 12 months he wants 6 listings to result from his DM system. With the goal established, he then decides the major steps that need to be created and then completed to achieve the desired outcome. For example, what kind of mailing piece (postcard or letter), how many pieces will be mailed, how often and when will the pieces be sent, and where will the mailings be sent to.

Then there are secondary decisions that need to be made. Who will print the mailing piece, who will mail it, and how will each mailing's

---

[1] A 'transaction side' is either the listing side or buyer side of a closed transaction. An agent who sells her own listing to her own buyer gets 2 sides.

effectiveness be measured? The frequency, quantity, timing, and locations all must be decided. All this is done as part of the planning process and far in advance of the first mailing.

Contrast that method with the one used by the agent who uses direct mail only when they run out of clients. There's no structure or consistency. It's only when they have no one to work with that they say, "I guess I'll send out some postcards". Then, when they fail to get a response (maybe because they mailed their listing solicitation postcard in mid-December) they decide direct mail doesn't work and try something else equally haphazardly. No wonder they struggle – they're just throwing darts in the dark. The sensible agent who chooses to utilize direct mail as one of her systems, knows on January 1 how many mailings she will use, how many mailing pieces she will send, where she will send them, and when she will send them, for the entire year. The only thing she may not know in advance is the message as that may depend on market conditions. She does not go about her business willy-nilly. She does not react to things happening. She makes things happen.

In creating your business plan you want to identify systems that will accomplish the objective and that you will do. It does you no good to include a system of cold calling if you wouldn't make a cold call if your life depended on it. A business plan built on faulty systems will not result in success. I believe most agents can achieve their goals with just 3 or 4 effective systems. I will cover systems in Part II.

After you have determined what you want to accomplish (your goals) and you know what you have to do to achieve your goals (your systems), next you have to ensure that you actually do what you have to do. You need a means of staying on track.

Some agents are very capable of doing this themselves. They are disciplined, detailed, and very aware of what they do and what they need to do. Less disciplined agents may have a spouse who is particularly effective at keeping them on track. Still others may need the help of a third-party to ensure they don't stray from the plan by chasing pretty butterflies.

Having goals and systems and not having a means of ensuring you stay on track will result in production less than if you have someone helping you. In some offices the broker or the manager can be part of that system. There are many professional coaches that can fill this role, too. The important thing is that the agent realizes that setting goals and determining systems is not enough. You need something (or someone) to keep you on your path – to protect you from the many distractions that are part of this job. I will cover this in Part III.

I hope the whole concept of developing your plan is exciting to you. It should be. For many years I worked as an agent without a plan with my income rising and falling seemingly beyond my control. When the market was good I made more money and when the market was bad I made less. But when I was introduced to the concept of a business plan and then incorporated it into my business I learned that I no longer had to be dependent on the market. I learned that if I knew what I wanted and how I could accomplish it, it was only a matter of following my plan and I would be successful. In subsequent years I have taught this concept to untold numbers of agents who have benefited from it. I trust you will benefit from it too.

Part I

Goals

One day Alice came to a fork in the road and saw a Cheshire cat in the tree.
"Which road do I take?" she asked.
"Where do you want to go?" was his response.
"I don't know" Alice answered.
"Then" said the cat, "it doesn't matter."

- From 'Alice's Adventures in Wonderland'
by Lewis Carroll

Before you can set off for a destination you need to know what that destination is. The trouble for many real estate agents is they have not thoughtfully considered where it is they want to go. They do not have a clear idea what they are trying to accomplish. Without a specific destination in mind, they wander, meander and drift, devoid of direction and enthusiasm. And they list and sell a fraction of the homes they are capable of.

If there is one aspect of the business plan that is more important than any other it is determining your goals. The more specific you are in determining meaningful goals, the more likely you will achieve them. Vague goals produce vague results. Specific goals result in specific results. Goals help provide direction. They motivate. If the goal is clear and has meaning to you, it will mobilize you to act in such a way as to accomplish it.

As I write this chapter sitting at my desk in my office, I can look up at a five-dollar bill that is tacked to the uppermost corner of my office. It is a visual I used for one of my agents. We pretended that rather than it being a five-dollar bill it was $50,000. I wanted to impress upon him the importance of having clear goals. $50,000 was important to him.

He wanted it. He needed it. But I told him to close his eyes before I tacked the money to the wall. I spun him around a bit and then said, "Go get it." Eyes still closed and not having a clue where the money was (much less how to get to it), he stumbled around, bumping into things and becoming frustrated. Because he could not see what he was pursuing, he struggled. He did not get to the five-dollar bill.

Then I told him to open his eyes. Now he could see where the thing he wanted was. But I wanted him to experience what pursuing a worthy goal is like in the real world so I stacked chairs in his way, obstructing his path. These obstacles presented a challenge, but because he could see the destination clearly, he was able to work his way around them. He plotted a course, taking into account those things that might keep him from getting the $50,000. Seeing that the money was above his reach, he also made plans to drag a chair over so he could stand on it and reach the money. He mobilized his resources. He overcame obstacles. He succeeded because he was able to fix his eyes on what he wanted.

The more real your goal is to you the more likely you will achieve it. The more you can see it, feel it, and taste it, the more effective it will be in guiding and motivating you.

I don't want to suggest that every real estate agent is motivated by money. Most are motivated by a need to provide the funds that enable them to live the standard of living they desire. But there are many agents – particularly those whose basic physical needs are already met - who are motivated by other things important to them, such as achieving what they consider a particular standard of excellence (50 transaction sides in a year, a company award designation, top 10 ranking in their marketplace, etc.). Many other agents are sufficiently motivated simply by doing better than the year before – even if it is just a single deal more. That's perfectly okay. Money is not the motivator for everyone. You need to identify what motivates you and develop your goals with that in mind. For most agents, the reason they work is to earn money to provide for their family so we will focus on how to use your financial need to move you to effective action.

In establishing your real estate goals, whether they are based on financial need or personal fulfillment, ultimately you are looking to determine exactly what level of real estate production you need to achieve. Selling a house in and of itself is not the goal. It is what that sale provides, i.e. money. But money also in and of itself is not the goal. What is the goal is the standard of living and the quality of life we want for ourselves and those that depend on us. Money is a means to the kind of life we want to live (or a means of keeping score for those who are motivated by non-monetary accomplishments) and real estate sales provides the money. Therefore, we need to figure out what level of real estate production will enable us to live the life we desire.

It starts with determining your need. When I refer to 'need' I mean how much money we need to earn, what will it cost us to live the kind of lifestyle we desire– things like food, shelter, gasoline, insurance, etc. We also want to quantify the cost for things we want. Things like a vacation home, a new car, a new TV – whatever is important to you that is not essential but desired.

We also have to understand what it costs to be in business. We pay fees to our broker, memberships in MLSs, office supplies, postage, etc. We need to know exactly what it costs to be in business.

Then there are taxes. Inasmuch as taxes are a function of your net income and varies depending on where you live, the tax figure is somewhat difficult to estimate. For the purposes of illustration, we'll assume a total tax rate of 20% of your net income. You can adjust it if necessary.

By taking how much it costs you to live and adding to it your business expenses as well as the things you want, and of course taxes, you will come up with the total amount of money you need to earn to live the life you want – 'The Grand Total' we can call it. If there is another source of income in your family (spouse income, investment income, etc.) you can deduct that from the 'Grand Total' to determine how much money you need to earn from your real estate sales business.

Once you know that number, you then want to translate that monetary need to the number of houses you need to list and sell. To do that you start by analyzing your past production. You look at what percentage of your business has been working with sellers versus buyers, what percentage of your listings sell, what has been your average sale price and commission, etc. If you are satisfied with this distribution between sellers and buyers and your average sale price, etc., you can move forward using those numbers as a guide. If you are not happy with your current business makeup (for example, you closed[2] 12 deals last year and 11 were with buyers), you decide now what you <u>want</u> it to be and use your desired mix rather than your historical mix.

When you are through you will know <u>exactly</u> how many listings you need to take, how many of them must close, and how many buyer deals you have to close. With this information, you will be able to move on to the second part of the real estate business plan – deciding on what systems you will use to create the relationships with sellers and buyers.

Before we can do that though, we need to know your monetary need. We'll start with your household budget. In Appendix A (pages 65-67) you will find a two-page spreadsheet labeled **Household Budget**. Fill in your expenses in such a way that will enable you live life the way you want to.

---

[2] I use the term 'closed' or 'closing' but other areas may use the terms 'settle' or 'settlement'. They mean the same thing, i.e. a completed sale/transaction.

Business Expenses

Now let's look at what it costs you to run your business.

Determining many of your expenses will be easy. If you know you will need 6 lawn signs you can look up the price in a catalog. Other business expenses may pose a challenge. For example, you may not know just yet what systems you are going to use so you may not be able to quantify how much money you will need for a direct mail program, open house program, or other system that will generate client opportunities. You may have to estimate at first and then refine your numbers once you know what systems you will use.

Another challenge may be in quantifying the cost of your broker. Most agents don't think of their broker as an expense, but in fact, the broker is usually the largest expense most agents have. If you start with the presumption that 100% of the commission on a closed transaction belongs to you (not your broker) and from which you pay a portion to your broker for the services he provides, you will realize that your broker is probably your largest expense.

For example, let's assume you are going to close something in the neighborhood of $85,000 in total commissions (the amount paid to your company at settlement) next year. If your split with your broker is you keep 60% and he keeps 40%, your broker cost is $34,000 ($85,000 x 40% = $34,000).

If you pay a franchise fee it is even more. Various fixed fees like errors and omissions insurance, technology fees, and transaction fees are easy to quantify but the percentage of each transaction your broker takes may require some side calculations.

Another challenge is some brokers offer a variable commission split where the agent gets a higher split once certain production thresholds are achieved. I suggest you assume a reasonable expectation of how much you will earn and calculate the cost of your broker according to the graduated scale. You can refine the figure later.

For example, if you are on a graduated scale where you keep 60% of the first $40,000, 65% of the next $20,000 and 70% of everything over $60,000, your cost would be $16,000 for the first $40,000 you closed, $7,000 for the next $20,000 you closed, and $7,500 for the remaining $25,000 in production. The total then would be $30,500.

(Remember this does not include franchise fees. They are a separate expense and must be listed as a separate expense.)

Use the budget sheet found in Appendix A (pages 69-71) labeled **Business Budget** to determine a reasonably accurate estimate of your business expenses. Some expenses like cell phone or gasoline can be accounted for in either your household or business budget. It doesn't really matter where these are entered because in the end they are all added up together. Those expenses that vary depending on your level of production (broker cost, franchise fees, transaction fees, etc.) can be changed in your budget once you know what your income goal is. It's probably best to use a pencil.

Things You Want But Do Not Need

On this spreadsheet you want to identify those things you want but that are not essential. Those things that are essential should appear on your household budget, but things like a special vacation, new car, boat, dinner out once a week, money for hobbies, etc., things you desire but do not need, are entered on this budget page.

Don't be shy about listing everything you want. Henry Ford said, "There is no man living who isn't capable of doing more than he thinks he can do." How will you ever achieve that which you have never done if you first don't identify exactly what it is you want? Forget whether you think you are capable; we'll address that later. Right now don't cheat yourself by aiming low.

One of the reasons you go through this budget process is to help determine what you want from your work efforts and the actions you need to take to earn the income you need to live the life you desire. Many agents simply accept what the market gives them. When the market is good they live well. When the market is bad they live poorly. By crafting a plan and then following that plan you can live the life you want to live irrespective of the market. You simply have to identify what you want, translate that into production quotas, identify the systems that will provide that level of business, and then get to work.

On the spreadsheet labeled **Desires** found in Appendix A (page 73), fill in everything you want. You can go back and modify it later, but for right now the sky's the limit. Write out exactly what you want even if you don't believe you can get it.

The Grand Total

If you have completely filled out the three budget sheets, you now know how much money you have to earn to pay your household expenses, your business expenses, get the things you want and pay your taxes. This is the cost to live your life the way you want to live it. Let's total it up.

Household Expenses		$ _____
Business Expenses	add	_____
Total Wants	add	_____
Estimated Taxes	add	_____
Total Need	Total	_____
Other Family Revenue	subtract	(_____)
Your Income Goal		_____

This number may initially be frightening, but don't despair. It may be more than you have ever earned, but that's not important. What is important is knowing what you need so you can plot a path to it with your systems.

Success Story:
Aiming High

I remember a particular time going through this process with one of my agents. When we calculated the total income she needed to fund her life the way she wanted it to be, the total came to about $185,000. She was visibly uncomfortable to learn this, as her best year previously had been $125,000.

This was the first year we worked together and her first time creating a business plan. She had never considered identifying what she wanted and figuring out a plan to achieve it. She just took what came her way.

When I did with her what we are going to do next, i.e. translate that income need into a production level, she relaxed and actually became encouraged because what she needed to do to reach her income goal, she felt, was within her ability. The number of dollars scared her but the number of transactions did not. We identified effective systems, she started working her plan, she met with me every two weeks to ensure she was staying on track, and that next year she earned nearly $250,000.

So let's figure out just how much real estate you need to sell. Before we do that however, we need to know a few things about your current business. To do that, we'll start by taking a look at your history.

How Are You Doing Business Now?

It is extremely beneficial to understand the specific aspects of your current business i.e. where your clients come from, your average sale price, the mix between listings and sales, what percentage of your listings sell, the average commission you receive, etc. This is all useful data.

If you are an experienced agent, you can use the past to help determine your future. One of the most fascinating exercises I go through with my agents is identifying the source of their prospects. I want them to know where their clients came from. By identifying the source of your clients you will be able to see what systems are working for you and what systems you are not utilizing. An agent who does all of her business with her sphere of influence is missing opportunities by not establishing new relationships via open houses, direct mail, or other proven ways of uncovering prospects.

> ### *What If You Are A New Agent?*
>
> *While having a history is useful in the planning process, it is not mandatory. You should be able to approximate your average sale price using data supplied by your local board of Realtors or your manager/broker.*

This information can also help you avoid mistakes. At one coaching session, one of my agents told me he was thinking of dropping his Internet advertising. The cost of $500/month was too much, he thought. I had no objection to him doing this – he can use any systems he wants – but I asked him to go over his most recent deals and how he met the client. He was amazed to learn that 8 deals in the previous 12 months had come from clients who found him as a result of his Internet advertising. We took it a step further and calculated that Internet advertising earned him more than $50,000 in income. That $6,000/year investment paid back more than 8 times the cost. Wisely he decided to continue with the Internet ad program.

Another benefit of knowing where your clients come from is it might reveal where you need to improve your skills. Let's say you spent $2,000 last year on direct mail yet failed to establish a single relationship with a buyer or seller. Obviously something is wrong. It could be your message, your timing, where you are mailing to, or something about your mailing piece.

Even when you do experience some success, a careful study of your results may reveal opportunities for improvement. For example, if you hosted 14 open houses last year and didn't close at least 6 sales, your open house system or technique needs help. By knowing where your clients are coming from you will be in a better position to measure your system's effectiveness and modify your systems if necessary.

Let's see what is working for you as well as where there are opportunities for improvement by learning where you clients come from. Use the spreadsheet in Appendix A (page 75) labeled **Listing Activity Recap** to identify where your listing leads came from over the previous 12 months. Be sure to include every seller, not just the ones you listed. We are analyzing your lead generation systems now – what works and what doesn't. Later you can analyze your effectiveness in converting these opportunities into listings. Right now we want to see how you are creating those opportunities.

To help, I've summarized the major sources of client opportunities:

1. **Sphere of Influence (SOI)** – Some call this your "book of business" but it actually is more than that. You may not have done business with someone who could still tell their friends about you. That's why you want to include anyone that knows you, even casually. Past clients, family members, friends from church, neighbors, parents of your children's friends, etc. If you know them and they know you, they are part of your sphere of influence.

2. **Direct Mail** – If you met them solely because you sent them something, label that prospect 'direct mail'. Even better is to identify what kind of mail, i.e. 'Just Listed/Just Sold card? Out of area owner letter? General solicitation ("Would you like to know what your home is worth" postcard, etc.)

3. **Open House** – These are the prospects you meet as a result of you hosting an open house. They could be buyers or sellers. If you send a letter to the neighborhood inviting them to your open house and they come, consider that an open house opportunity, not a direct mail opportunity.

4. **Expired** – No matter what means you used to initiate the relationship, if they were an expired listing and you reached out to them, they belong in this category.

5. **For Sale By Owners** - The same as expireds. If they were a FSBO and you reached out to them, label them "FSBO".

6. **Referrals** – What I mean by 'referral' is a specific, broker-to-broker referral, not a lead that comes from a friend. A lead from a friend would be categorized as sphere of influence.

7. **Ad Response** - You put an ad in the newspaper (not an open house ad – that would be an open house lead) and someone calls you.

8. **Internet Ad Response** – The same as #7 but from the Internet. Be sure to differentiate between paid leads and someone simply seeing your listing online and then reaching out to you.

9. **Sign Calls** – Besides properly identifying the source of those that you met as a result of your lawn sign, knowing this number will provide powerful evidence to sellers you work for that don't want a sign.

10. **Seminars** – Do you host informational seminars? The people that come to one (excepting those in your sphere of influence that were specifically invited to your seminar) should be in this category.

11. **Cold Calling** – If you called someone cold, i.e. you were not told to call them by a mutual friend, label them "cold call".

12. **Door Knocking** – Like cold calling, door knocking isn't practiced like it once was, but if you do it, be sure to identify those opportunities as such.

13. **Other** – Make a new category for any specific event or activity you may have used in an attempt to create new relationships – Took a booth at a local home show? Sponsored a little league team? Bought an ad in your daughter's marching band yearbook? Wore your name badge and someone asked you "How's the real estate market?" Any deliberate action you used to create new opportunities should be identified and accounted for.

Don't skip or rush through this process. The information gathered from this exercise will be revealing and very profitable.

Now let's do the same thing with your buyers. Use the spreadsheet in Appendix A (page 77) labeled **Buyer Activity Recap**. Pay careful attention to the source of your buyers. Be sure to differentiate between a buyer who reaches out to you in response to an Internet property ad and one who reaches out to you due to an Internet personal branding ad. List every buyer you talked to in the last 12 months. (Note: Do not include every visitor to your open houses on this log. Many visitors to open houses have no interest in buying or selling and as such are not 'buyers' for our purposes here. You should analyze open house effectiveness separately. For now, just include open house visitors you actually form a relationship and begin working with).

Most agents also earn some income from activities other than sales and listings. They may do rentals, broker price opinions, or provide consulting services. So we have a true picture of your present business, use the form entitled **Other Revenue Recap** (page 79) to list your income from these non-sale related activities.

Finally, let's put all your statistical data concerning your business on a single page. I've provided an easy worksheet that will tell you at a glance the most important statistical information about your present business, i.e. how many transactions, your average sale price, how many sides were listings, etc. This may take a little time and require some digging on your part, but it will give you a starting point from which you can proceed. You will find the worksheet entitled, **Your Current Business** located in Appendix A (page 81).

Now We Look Forward

To this point we have spent time looking at your past production, and the source of that business. Now it is time to make some decisions about your future. You know how your business has been allocated between listings and buyers. At this point you want to ask yourself if this allocation is what you want it to be. For example, listings may have comprised only 20% of your closed transactions. If you want the allocation between listing and buyers to be something different, now is the time to recognize that. Soon we will be deciding which systems you will be using to initiate new relationships. Your choice of systems will be based, in part, on your listing/buyer mix.

Another consideration is your average price. Is it what you want it to be? If it is, there's nothing you need to do. But if you want to work with a more expensive market, you need to be deliberate in your systems planning.

Take a minute to read how one agent nearly doubled her average sale price in less than two years.

Success Story:
Changing Your Product Mix

I was fortunate to have a terrific agent join my company many years ago. She was already a great producer selling more than 40 homes/year, but most of these homes were low-priced condos. She was working hard but not making much money. She wanted to move into a more expensive market, so as part of her plan, she deliberately directed her energy and prospecting dollars into more expensive areas. She chose more upscale neighborhoods for her mailings and open houses. Soon her lawn signs began popping up in these more expensive neighborhoods.

She was successful transitioning to higher priced homes because a) she recognized that she was underutilizing her resources selling inexpensive condos, b) she was deliberate in her planning, and c) she was disciplined in the execution of her plan. Interestingly, a few years later she set her sights on an even higher priced market and again successfully made the transition. She knew what she wanted (because she constantly analyzed her business) and she was deliberate in her planning and execution.

Once you know what you want your business mix to be and the price range you want to work in, you are now ready to convert your financial goal to real estate production goals. To do that, use the form found in Appendix A (page 83) labeled, **Calculating Your Production Goals.**

You now know your income goal, your listings goal and your buyer closings goal. These numbers should be on the tip of your tongue all the time. They should be etched in your brain. These are your numbers – memorize them.

Congratulate Yourself –
You've Just Joined an Exclusive Club

Do you know how many real estate agents can tell you exactly what their goals are? The number is incredibly small. That you know your goals is a HUGE accomplishment. Here's a story that will illustrate why.

The great sales trainer, Zig Ziglar, tells of an Olympic champion archer. Zig said that he (Zig) could beat this Olympian at archery every time. Pausing for effect, Zig added, "Of course I'd have to blindfold the man and spin him around a few times ".

The story got a laugh every time Zig told it, and the audience got Zig's point - How can someone hit a target he cannot see?

But Zig was not done. The more powerful lesson came when he posed the question, "Of course you can't hit a target you cannot see. But how can you hit a target *that doesn't even exist?*"

The answer is, 'You can't'. But that is how most agents go about their business day-to-day, week-to-week, month-to-month, and year-to-year. They wander and drift and waste time, money, and energy. They do this because they don't have a target – they don't know what they are aiming at.

But you know what you are aiming at and it's a big deal. Congratulate yourself.

What If You Think, "I Can't Do That Many Sales"?

At this point in the planning process a problem may arise. What if you believe the production necessary to reach your goals is simply beyond what you are able (or willing) to do?

While anything is possible, you need to be realistic. If your needs and wants require you to sell 50 houses a year and you have never sold more than 10, you might have to reevaluate your plan. Here are a couple things you can do:

1. **Alter Your Product Mix** – If you are basing your revenues on an average sale price of $200,000, can you increase that number to $300,000? Remember that moving to a different price mark requires deliberate action that would need to be reflected in your systems.

2. **Do Business in a Different Way** – You may want to consider creating a team and being the leader and rainmaker leveraging the efforts of others for your benefit.

3. **Change Your Fee Structure** - If your level of service will support it, you may be able to close fewer deals if you get paid more on each deal.

4. **Cut Expenses** – Analyze your budgets. Are there expenditures that are not necessary? If so, cut them out. Remember, a dollar not spent is a dollar that goes right to your bottom line. Be careful however. Don't go slashing expenses that create opportunities.

5. **Reevaluate Your Goals** – If you've done everything you can and it still hasn't resulted in production goals you think are attainable, the only thing left to do is eliminate items from you needs to lower your income requirement.

Let's assume you believe the production you need to do is within your ability. You are now ready to move to the second part of a business plan – deciding what systems you will use to initiate client relationships that will result in you achieving those goals.

Part II

Systems

*"It is not enough to do your best.
You must know what to do and then do your best."*

- W. Edward Deming

The origin of every successful real estate transaction is some action or actions that result in you uncovering a prospect. Sometimes it is as easy as answering your phone and having the caller say, "You don't know me, but you sold the house for my friend. Can you help me as well?" Other times it involves exhaustive research, effort, and money.

Initiating new relationships with potential clients is Job #1 for the real estate salesperson. You can be spectacular showing houses, the world's best negotiator, and the Olympic champion in doing listing presentations, but if you don't have someone to do these things for you won't make a single sale. The work dedicated to developing new relationships is called prospecting and it is the most important thing the real estate agent must do.

There are many ways to initiate relationships with people interested in buying and selling real estate. Here are some examples of methods that primarily create listing opportunities:

- Contacting For Sale By Owners
- Contacting owners of listings that expired
- Cold Calling
- Direct Mail (when sent to homeowners)

Here are methods that primarily create buyer opportunities:

- Internet advertising
- Direct Mail (when sent to renters)
- Print advertising of your listings

Some methods create both buyer and listing opportunities. Here are some examples:

- Open Houses
- Your Sphere of Influence
- Informational seminars (depending on your subject – A Homebuyer's Seminar will attract buyers while a 'How To Prepare Your Home So It Sells at the Highest Price' will attract sellers)

Each of these methods can be broken down into individual steps which, taken together, comprise the system. Earlier I outlined the direct mail system. Let's look at another one – leveraging your sphere of influence.

Your sphere of influence is simply the network of people you know. They know you but they may not think of you as a real estate professional. You want them, when the topic of real estate comes up, to always think of you, so you employ a system to make them aware of your standing as a real estate agent. The system may look something like this:

1. Create a list of at least 200 names of people who know you. The list must have their name, address, phone number, and email address. (Note: As you build your list you may wonder if you should include people you are

certain will never sell their home. The answer is 'yes'! Put them on your list. You are looking to tap into their sphere of influence as well as your own. They may know someone who needs to sell or buy and will gladly recommend you.)

2. 12 times a year you will send a direct mail piece to your SOI to remind them of what you do. The mailings will be sent on the following schedule:

- January 15 – Just Sold postcard
- February 14 – Just Sold postcard
- March 12 – Letter expressing needs for listings
- April 12 – Just Sold postcard
- May 13 – Just Sold postcard
- June 15 – Invitation to customer appreciation event
- July 17 – Newsletter highlighting customer appreciation event
- August 13 – Invitation for comparative market analysis
- September 12 – Just Sold postcards
- October 14 – Just Sold post
- November 13 – Just Sold postcard
- December 10 – New Year calendar

3. Twice a year call them. One of the calls can be to invite them to your customer appreciation event. The other call can just be to say, "Hi, I was thinking about you. How's your family?" Before ending the call you can also ask, "I have a buyer who is looking for something very specific. So far they haven't seen anything they like. Do you know anyone thinking of selling?"

4. Host a customer appreciation event. This could be renting a movie theater and showing a family movie, hosting an 'Apple Pie' party just before Thanksgiving (where everyone gets a pie), having a pool party at your home, or anything else that is festive. A relatively small percentage of your SOI group will attend, but that's fine. The fact that you invited everyone is the important thing.

5. Email a flyer for a new listing with a note asking if they know anyone who might like your new listing. You will want to send this on schedule so the email arrives between the other mailings that arrive in their mailbox.

Your past successes and common wisdom will determine what the steps of your system are – this is just an example – but it shows the level of detail you want in devising your system.

The next step is to determine the cost of your system. In our SOI example the cost breakdown will be as follows:

Annual Cost of Monthly Mailing	$1,200.00
Annual Calendar Mailing	$750.00
Client Appreciation Event	$1,250.00
Monthly Email Messages	$0.00
Phone Calls	$0.00
Total Estimated Cost	$3,200.00

Finally you want to determine the revenues and profits this system will provide by estimating how many transactions your SOI system will provide. You can use your history as a guide or simply estimate. If you are using your history and have never systematically worked your SOI in the past, be sure to bump the historical figure upwards. Being deliberate in leveraging your SOI will yield significantly more opportunities.

Estimated # of Listings From SOI	8
Listings Closed	7
Buyer Sides Closed	6
Total Transaction Sides	13
Average Revenue/Side	$6,500
Estimated Total Revenue	$84,500
Expenses	$3,200
Profit	**$81,300**

It is important to calculate the anticipated profit for each of your systems. One reason is you want to be sure you are employing profitable systems. You could hire skywriters to spell out your name for all to see – and it might get you a listing – but if you pay $7,000 to get a $5,000 paycheck, it's not good. You want to always be aware of profit.

Another reason you want to calculate profit for each system is you want to take a 'long view' of the system. The long view is an extended view that takes into account that, from time to time, one portion of the system may not generate any opportunities, but taken over time all of them will generate enough to warrant using the system in the first place.

A good example of this is your open house program. Some open houses are a bust. No one comes. That's just the way it is. If you don't have the long view of the system you might be tempted to scrap the system. That would be a mistake. Evaluate the system over an extended period of time and not a single instance. If you are employing proven systems, sometimes your actions will yield results and other times they will not, but taken as a whole, the system will be effective and profitable.

As you develop your systems you may realize that some systems can be implemented with little involvement from you. Using our SOI system as an example, obviously you have to make the phone calls and you have to host the customer appreciation event, but the mailing portion can be handled by an assistant, freeing you to do other things.

No matter which systems you select to be part of your plan, there are certain things you want spelled out clearly:

1. The title of the system
2. Frequency
3. Outline of activities
4. Expected results
5. Cost
6. Timetable
7. Expected return on investment

For example, here's what an open house system might look like:

Title – 'Open House System'. It will be used to help initiate new relationships with sellers and buyers.

Frequency - Host 16 open houses in the next 12 months (specific dates to be determined but the # of open houses each month will be as follows)

- January – 1
- February -1
- March – 3
- April – 3
- May - 2
- June – 1
- July/August – 0
- September – 2
- October -2
- November – 1
- December – 0

Method - For each open house I will do the following

- Select subject house two weeks in advance
- Submit ad to newspaper – Monday
- Update listing with open house date - Monday
- Place 'Open House This Sunday' sign rider on the lawn sign the Monday before
- Send letters of invitation to 40 neighbors on Wednesday
- Verify owner will not be home Sunday afternoon – Wednesday
- Send email to buyer database inviting them to open house, Thursday and Saturday
- Have printed materials ready – Friday
- Social media posts – Sunday morning
- Place directional signs – Sunday morning
- Arrive at house – Sunday 30 minutes ahead of start time
- Turn on every light, check the house for cleanliness
- Eat energy bar and stay hydrated – 30 minutes prior
- Be the perfect host
- Clean up
- Remove sign rider
- Talk to owner with results
- Follow up appropriately with interested parties
- Add names of visitors to database for future contact

Targeted Results

# of Open Houses Hosted	16
Average # of Visitors/Open House	8
Total Expected Visitors - Annual	128
Listing Opportunities	8
Listings Taken	6
Listing Sides Closed	5
Buyer Sides Closed	6
Total Closed Sides	11
Estimated Revenue/Side	$6,500.00
Estimated Total Revenue	$71,500.00
Estimated Cost ($75/Open House)	$1,200.00
Profit	**$70,300.00**

Planning out a year in advance will help you overcome the urge to ditch a system that doesn't yield results right away. Agents do this all the time. They do an open house, nobody comes, they decide open houses don't work and never do one again. Big mistake.

Even the most expertly executed open house program requires that you understand that every open house is not going to pay off. Using our example, we are going to do 16 open houses and we have budgeted 11 opportunities. That means we are going to have no tangible successes in at least five of our open houses. That's to be expected – no one gets a hit every time they step to the plate. But just because you strike out once (or twice or more) that doesn't mean you don't get up to bat again. You simply review your performance, make any needed adjustments, and keep with your plan. No system works every time. You just have to stay at it. Your systems budget will help you remember this.

With the help of a coach or your broker/manager you should be able to devise specific systems – step-by-step processes – for each of your lead generation activities. Use a chart similar to the sample on the next page to plan where your business will come from and then use the **Systems Summery** worksheets found in Appendix A (pages 87-93) to outline the systems you will use in your business. I've included four.

How Do You Estimate How Many Opportunities Each System Will Provide?

Your systems goals will come partly from experience and partly from your own expectations. Experience says that every person that walks in my open house is not going to buy or list with me. In fact most won't. But if I'm going to invest time and money in this system I am going to do everything in my power to get results. The targets may be somewhat arbitrary (though certainly reasonable), but once I've set them, my focus and efforts are going to be on achieving those objectives. Just by identifying the target I am taking a major step towards reaching that target. Just remember, 'See it – Believe It – Go Get It'

Sample Budgeted Distribution of Client Source

System	Listings*	Buyer Sides
Sphere of influence	8	6
Direct Mail	6	1
Open House	4	4
Expireds	4	0
FSBO	0	0
Cold Call	0	0
Broker Referrals	2	0
Paid Internet Ads	1	6
Seminars	0	0
Other-	0	0
Other-	0	0
Other-	0	0
Other-	0	0
Total	25	17

*80% of listings will sell - 20 x $6,500/listing = $130,000
Buyer side revenue = 17 x $6,500/buyer side =   110,500
Total Revenue   **$240,500**

Let's stop here for a moment and recap what you have done so far.

- You learned how much money it will take to pay all your bills – business and personal
- You know the cost of the things you want but don't necessarily need
- You have translated that monetary need into real estate production figures – total transaction sides, listings, buyer sides
- You have allocated the source of those listings and buyer sides to one of several systems that you will employ to create the opportunities.

In sum, you know where you are going and you know how to get there. Now you have to be certain you do what you know you must. This leads us to the final aspect of a real estate agent's business plan – developing a means of staying on track.

Part III

Staying on Track

"If I had a dollar for every time I was distracted,
I wish I had a puppy."

- Unknown

Most people don't know how a GPS works – the mathematics that is – but we all know what a GPS does. When you put a destination address into the GPS it creates a route (plan) for you to follow. As you proceed, it is constantly checking your location in relation to that route. If you venture off that route, it interrupts you to let you know you're astray and tells you how to get back on track. It is a great invention and I wonder how we ever got along without it. Think of the lost time, the stress, and the lost opportunities in your life if, instead of being where you wanted to be, you were somewhere else, wandering around, lost.

Stressed, wandering around, and lost – words that can be used to describe many real estate agents. Real estate agents need something like a GPS. I'm not aware of any GPS device for the real estate industry, but there are several tools you can use that will help you realize when you have gone off track and then get you back on the right path.

Earlier I wrote that there are some agents who are determined, disciplined and very capable of keeping themselves on track. For them it is useful to have some kind of accounting software or even a simple

> *The key to staying on track is recognizing that going off track is a very real and potentially damaging reality.*

spreadsheet to remind them of what they have to do and whether or not they are doing it. Keeping track of your open house program, direct mail program, approaches to for sale by owners and expireds all serve the purpose of reminding you what you're supposed to do.

Keeping detailed records of your activities provides another benefit in that it will provide data for you for future planning activities. For example, a year of doing open houses will give you a good idea how many visitors you greet, how many of them turn into clients and how much your open house system is worth. The same benefit applies to mailings, Internet ad expenditures, and any other aspect of your business. My mentor and coach, Floyd Wickman is fond of saying "If it is worth doing it is worth measuring".

Technology offers many means of recording our activities and you should choose those that work for you. Even a simple spreadsheet on paper can be useful. In Appendix B (pages 99-107) I have included several very simple spreadsheets to help you stay on track. You can easily design new ones that work for you.

Another useful means of staying on track is what I call the "30 Second Time Out". The name, 30-second time out, is taken from the National Football League. At some point during the game, the coach will call a '30 second time out'. It is a brief stoppage of the game to allow the players to catch their breath, evaluate where they are, and decide what to do next.

In the same way, taking a short break to meet with your broker or manager can help you stay on track. I meet with several of my agents, 1-on-1, on a regular basis just to review their business and make sure they are not straying from their plan. These are not accountability meetings and there is no pain or embarrassment. We simply take a snapshot of their current business – production and activities – and compare that to where the plan says the agent should be. An added bonus of these meetings is that our discussions often lead to solutions to particular challenges, as well as ideas for new ways for the agent to grow her business. If you have a broker or manager that is skilled at asking the right questions, and is willing to give you the time, a meeting with them 30 to 45 minutes once or twice a month will help keep you on track.

That same benefit can be achieved even if your broker or manager is not willing or capable of meeting with you. There are dozens of very capable real estate coaches who will not only keep you on track but also introduce other systems or modifications to your current systems that might prove profitable. In choosing a coach you want someone you respect but that also does not intimidate you. You want to be comfortable and view the coach as a tool to help you, not someone to be feared. You can find professionals skilled in helping agents by searching the Internet using the search term, 'real estate coaches'. There will be an expense and it won't be small, but the value of staying on track, as well as the other suggestions, systems refinements, and support your coach will provide make it well worth the investment.

The key to staying on track is recognizing that going off track is a very real and potentially damaging reality. Sometimes we get lazy, sometimes a prettier butterfly comes into our life, and sometimes life just gets in the way and draws us away from those activities that we know we should be doing. Many times just keeping up with managing the details of our successes - our listings and ongoing transactions - takes us off our path. To conduct your business believing that you will not have wrong turns and potholes along the way is naïve and damaging. It is not a matter of if you will be distracted; it is a matter of when you will be distracted and how damaging it will be. You can have the clearest vision of what you want and know specifically what you need to do to accomplish it, but if you don't plan for the unpredictable it is easy to drift off your plan and then find yourself lost. How many times have you said to yourself on Friday afternoon, "Where did this week go? I got nothing accomplished."

Weeks become months and months become years and we wonder why we feel we are stuck in a rut. In fact, it is a rut of our own choosing. When we fail to be proactive in the management of our business, we have no one but ourselves to blame for the outcome.

Be prepared for the unexpected. It is going to happen. What you need to do is recognize when you're getting off track and then take the appropriate steps to get back on track. If you can do this on your own, great. If you can't, get the help of your broker or manager. If they can't do it hire a coach.

You may be familiar with a commercial on TV for an investment firm that offers a great visual for illustrating the importance of staying on track. They use a green line to signify your retirement plan. They say if you stay on the green line you will reach your retirement goals. It is the same for your real estate business goals– draw the line and then stay on it.

Part IV

Pulling It All Together

"Grain by grain – a loaf; stone upon stone – a palace."

- George Bernard Shaw

Your business plan is a document that sets the vision of where you are going and the means to get there. It's your roadmap, guiding you so your business reaches its destination (profitability) successfully. But what does the document look like? How is it created? What do you do with it once you have in hand?

The document is personal in nature and as such can be created in many ways to suit different personalities. But there are some things common to every effective plan. In this section we'll go through the process of actually putting a plan together - step-by-step - that is a usable tool that will guide you for the next 12 months.

We'll begin with the question, "Where should you do the actual activities associated with creating your plan?" I'll answer that first by saying where you don't do this. You don't do it in front of the TV. You don't do it at the kitchen table amidst all the activities of your family. You don't do it in five-minute time blocks in between taking phone calls at your desk. Instead, you want to shut off your phone, go to a quiet place where you can relax, and consider what you want and how you're going to go about getting it. Some agents go away for a weekend. It is not a vacation but it does involve removing themselves from the busyness of their days so they can relax and allow thoughts and ideas that would otherwise be crowded out by the demands of everyday life the chance to be heard. If you have the resources to go away, that's great, but you can also do this at home. Just remove yourself to a place of quiet where you won't be distracted. You don't have to do your plan in a single sitting but you want to be certain that anytime you spend compiling the plan is time you are 100% focused on the plan.

The data you need to make your plan can be pulled together in the days and weeks prior to the time you actually create your plan. You should have your checkbook, any previous budgets, summary sheets that you would provide your accountant, and any other financial information. You also want a detailed record of your production for the previous 12 months. You should be able to get without difficulty from your broker or through the MLS. Once you have everything in hand, follow these steps to create your plan.

1. Fill out the **Household Budget** sheet (page 65-67). This is where having your checkbook is useful, not only to provide accurate information but to remind you of an expense you may have forgotten.

2. Fill out the **Business Budget** sheet (page 69-71). As I expressed earlier, this may be difficult because some of your expenses are a function of your production. For example, the amount you pay to your broker or your franchise fee. You should estimate what your production will be and calculate the cost based on that production. You can go back and make adjustments if the production objective is higher or lower than what you assumed.

3. Fill in the budget sheet for **Desires** (page 73). Be bold with this. Many agents accept ordinary when spectacular is available to them just by reaching a little farther. Don't limit yourself to what you think you can achieve. Instead, create the vision of what you want.

4. Calculate your estimated taxes. This is another variable that may need adjustment later but if you assume 15%-20% of your net income you will be reasonably close. Check with your accountant for a more accurate figure.

5. Take the totals from steps 1-4 and determine the **Grand Total** (page 85). This is the amount of money you need to earn. If there is additional income in your family like a spouse who works, investment income, etc., subtract that from the Grand Total. What you are left with is the amount of money you need to make from your real estate sales business.

6. The next step is to determine the details of your current production. To do that, use the form entitled **Your Current Business** (page 81). You don't have to do your business next year the same way you did it this year but it is helpful to know what you did do this year as a guide. Spend time considering the results from this analysis. Ask yourself if you are happy with the number of transactions you closed, the mix between listings and sales, your average sale price, and your average commission earned. Many agents in the pursuit of what they enjoy don't always realize the inefficiencies in their work. Here's an example from my own experience.

I love listing properties. I love the entire process, from uncovering the listing opportunity to doing the listing presentation to getting the seller's commitment. Like many agents I derive energy from the challenge and the success of listing. But sometimes I lose sight of the end goal in pursuit of the listing. I got a referral one time for a large mobile home in my marketplace. It was a listing so I was excited. I met the homeowner, took the listing, felt self-satisfied, but then as I was driving back to my office, I calculated the amount of the small fee I would earn. In the end I didn't lose money because the mobile home did sell and I was paid a fee, but in another sense I did lose because my time could have been used more profitably. When you do this evaluation you may be surprised to see how many opportunities you had to work more effectively.

Decide if your product mix is correct and if it is not, decide what you want it to be going forward.

7. Now it is time to translate your income need into actual real estate production, i.e. the number of listings and sales. You do this with the form, **Calculating Your Production Goals** (page 83) using the numbers for average sale price, commission, etc., you calculate how many listings you need, how many of them need to sell, and how many buyer deals you must close. These are your numbers. They are important. You should take several 3 x 5 cards and write your numbers on them. Post them where you will see

them every day. One place may be on the mirror in your bathroom. Another may be on the dashboard of your car. One certainly should be on your desk. In time you won't consciously see these numbers but subconsciously you will. Even though you won't be aware of it, just having those numbers in front of you will cause them to be part of your life, part of who you are. Your subconscious will then direct your activities so that you become what it believes you to be.

8. With the numbers in place, now it is time to decide which systems you are going to use. I recommend that you use no more than five. It is better to be effective at 3 or 4 systems than to be ineffective at 7. By diluting your efforts doing multiple systems inefficiently you may feel you are working, but you will not be achieving. I would go so far as to say you should start with three systems, work to do them expertly and once you have perfected them, add others.

One system that should be in every agent's plan is a system for leveraging his or her sphere of influence. You want to be certain that the people that know you and trust you, know you are a real estate professional. Another system that should be in every agent's plan is a direct mail system. It can be something as simple as Just Listed and Just Sold cards announcing your recent successes, or as complex as a massive mailing to every homeowner in your marketplace, but every great agent uses direct mail. The other systems you decide to use should be selected based on their effectiveness, your budget, and your willingness to work them. I have enclosed several blank **System Summary** forms (pages 89-95) for you to identify the systems you will use.

9. By this point you know your production goals and you now know what systems are going to use. Next you want to allocate those deals and listings to the individual systems in your plan. This is an inexact science but as I indicated earlier, simply by writing the number down you have taken a major step in achieving that goal. You can use your history as a guide or you can just use common sense, but you want to source each of your deals to a specific system. You can enter these objectives/expectations in the area indicated on the **Business Plan Summary** sheet (page 87).

10. The third component of your business plan is your means for staying on track. In Appendix B (page 97) I have included several accounting sheets for various systems you may employ. You can use these or any of your own design. The important thing is that you measure your work. Another

tool for staying on track may be meeting regularly with your broker. Now is the time to decide that as well as when you meet, for example, the 1st and 3rd Mondays at 9 AM. Don't leave this detail out. You want your plan to be specific.

Your plan may include a 30-minute review and planning period every Sunday night. Put that in your calendar as part of your plan to stay on track.

Every aspect of your plan can be summarized on the **Business Plan Summary**. This form includes all the information I've covered so far plus a place for you to identify professional development goals. Here you may want to list things like earning a professional designation, reinventing your listing presentation, taking a leadership position in the Board of Realtors®, etc. This single page 'Business Plan Summary' sheet will be the cover of your business plan. At a glance you will be able to see every component of your plan.

How you put together the papers of your plan is up to you but I suggest that immediately after the Business Plan Summary sheet you have the pages for your systems followed by the accountability sheets that correspond to those systems. After that I would place the record of closings so you can track your progress and behind that your budgets, calculation forms, recap forms, and any note sheets you scribbled on in the creation of the plan. All told your plan should run between 10 and 20 pages. Make a copy to be filed for future use. One copy should be on your desk at all times. A third copy should travel with you in your briefcase.

This is one way to organize your actual planning document but not the only way. Do what works best for you. The important thing is that you recognize your plan is a vital tool for your success. It should be as much a part of your business as your phone or computer. You should be touching it every day. You don't want to make the mistake of creating a wonderful plan then filing it away, never to see it again while you go on doing business as you always have.

In Appendix C (page 107) you will find a sample of a finished business plan. Use it as a guide in creating your own.

Afterword

"In preparing for battle, I have always found that plans are useless but planning is indispensable."

- Dwight D. Eisenhower

I don't believe the former president meant to be taken literally when he said plans are useless. The architect of the D-Day invasion knew very well that plans are useful and essential. I believe what he meant was that the process of creating the plan is the greatest benefit of a plan. That compared to the plan itself, the process of determining what you want to accomplish, understanding why you want to accomplish it, and setting a course is far more beneficial than the actual plan itself.

Considering your goals causes you to identify what really is important in your life. You first have to make sure your basic needs are met, but then you can expand from 'needs' to 'wants'. The real benefit comes when you realize – and not everyone gets this right away (in fact some never do) - that you don't have to accept mediocre. You don't have to content yourself with what 'fate' may send your way. If you are clear about what you want, if it is important to you, and if you are willing to work to get it, you can accomplish almost anything.

With your destination clearly established, you then need to decide what activities will advance you towards your destination. You do this by understanding what systems are effective and then committing to perfecting those systems. You become a student of your trade and dedicate yourself to excellence. You map out your year, quarter, month, and day and then get to work.

Along the way there will be distractions. Distractions are to the real estate agent what kryptonite is to Superman and the bucket of water was to the Wicked Witch of the West. Distractions are an agent's downfall. They rob you of time, money, and energy and usually leave you wanting. The first step in not falling victim to distractions is being aware that they are all around you and knowing they have the power to consign you to a life of want and mediocrity. Do not make the mistake of thinking you will not be affected by distractions. They are insidious. They move in like a slow fog, imperceptible at first, then, before you know it, you are wandering around, lost.

> **What If I Get An Opportunity But It Wasn't From One Of My Systems - Should I Ignore It?**
>
> *If you have set meaningful goals and established effective systems that, properly executed, will result in you attaining your goals, you want to be very careful about deviating from your plan. The best plan in the world will do you no good if you don't stay at it. But if you are certain you are not just chasing after a 'pretty butterfly' and you are not neglecting your work on your systems, there's no harm in working to capitalize on an unexpected opportunity.*

You must combat distractions by putting in place a means of staying on track. Whether it is a monthly meeting with your manager or broker, a weekly call to your coach, or just you faithfully recording your activities, you need to account for your activities and results. You need to be aware that you may need to make adjustments. If you don't do what the GPS does, i.e. check your progress against the goal – you will never be aware you are off track and you won't recognize the need to make adjustments.

Most agents are Type A personalities – self-starting go-getters. Sitting thoughtfully considering the various aspects of their business and recording results of mailings, open houses, etc. doesn't seem like work to them. They would rather be 'doing something productive'. But keeping track of your activities and results is doing something productive. In fact, it is doing something very important. The feedback you get from monitoring your systems will guide you in refining those systems, learning where you need to improve, and limiting lost time and money. Sitting at your desk filling out spreadsheets is time well spent.

The Most Difficult Question Every Real Estate Agent Must Ask

You may have never considered the importance of business planning but inherently you do know it is important, as this illustration I am about to share will prove.

Imagine you are a shareholder in a company and that company has been underperforming. Competitors are taking market share, the stock price is flat, and management seems content with the status quo. You have most of your life savings invested in that company so you decide to go to the annual meeting to hear what leadership has to say. During the question-and-answer period you get up and ask the people on stage, "What is your plan for increasing profitability?"

The CEO says they haven't really given it much thought. "Haven't really given it much thought", you think to yourself incredulously.

You still have the microphone so you ask, "What are the company's objectives for the next 12 months?"

"We really don't have any objectives" the CEO explains, "We are going to take things as they come."

"Really!" you think, then you ask the CEO, "I've been reading on line about the plans your competitors have and they seem very specific and detailed. You're confident that not having specific plans will result in maximum shareholder profitability?"

"Well we hope so. Who knows what the future holds?" the leader of the company you are deeply invested in says.

How long do you think it would take for you to call your investment manager to sell all your stock in that aimless company and put it into some other company? You wouldn't dream of investing in an operation that doesn't have clearly defined goals and a plan for accomplishing those goals.

Yet real estate agents do this every day. You are the company and you and your family and the people who depend on you are the major shareholders.

Imagine your daughter at your company's shareholders meeting asking you "What is your plan for increasing profitability?" Would you answer, "I'm not really sure, I haven't given it much thought." Your son asks you, "Mom what are your objectives for the next 12 months?" Can you imagine saying to him, "I don't have any objectives. I'm just going to hope for the best."

If you are a real estate agent you own a business. You are an entrepreneur, not an employee. You don't get a salary. You don't get a paid vacation. You don't have company-provided health insurance. You, not someone else, is responsible for your business's success. You are the majority stockholder in your company. Those that depend on you are shareholders. Your focus should be on increasing shareholder value. You do that by growing your business and you grow your business by first identifying what you want to accomplish, deciding how you are going to go about accomplishing it, and then ensuring that you execute faithfully.

You don't have to do this. You can simply take what comes your way. But the real estate sales business is extremely competitive and astute agents understand that efficient agents can more easily take a far larger share of the business than in any time in history. As an agent's business grows she has more resources to invest in the business and make it grow even more. The popularity of teams has allowed agents to multiply their effectiveness and influence. Technology has allowed for relatively small operations (even single agents) to approach and then stay in contact with thousands and thousands of potential homeowners and homebuyers.

> *Would you invest in your business knowing the way your business is run?*

The disparity between agents who thrive and agents that struggle will continue to get greater and greater. In my marketplace there are about 1,000 agents that have closed at least 1 transaction in the last 12 months. The top 10 agents of this group closed more transaction sides than the bottom 500 agents did! Imagine, a group of agents that could fit in a van sold more houses than another group that would fill an auditorium.

The sad part is the agents who just take things as they come are not even aware of the opportunities they never see. That neighbor, who lists with another agent, didn't do so because she didn't want to list with her. In fact the homeowners might have listed her home with her if she had thought to. But they listed with someone else because the other agent – working from a plan and using resources earned as a result of previous planning – was far more visible to them via monthly postcards, Internet ads, 'for sale' signs around town, and enthusiastic reviews from friends - every one the result of a system the agent created and then implemented.

The most effective action an agent at any level of production can do to grow her business is to create and then follow an effective business plan. It starts with establishing clear goals, continues with the creation of effective systems, and is dependent on a means of ensuring those systems are executed.

You can have the business you want. You can have the life you want. You just need a plan.

Appendix A

Planning Forms

Household Budget
(page 1)

Home

	Monthly Cost	Annual Cost
Housing (Rent/Mortgage)	$ 850	$ 10,200
Property Taxes	0	
Heating Oil/Gas	150	~~2,800~~ 1,800
Electric	100	1,200
Homwowners Insurance	0	
Lawn Service	0	
Snow Removal	0	
Home Improvements	0	
Water/Sewer	0	
Other	20	240
Other		
Total Home	$	$

Daily Living

	Monthly Cost	Annual Cost
Food	$ 400	$ 4,800
Car Payments	0	
Car Maintainence	50	600
Gasoline	200	2,400
Auto Insurance	500	6,000
Health Insurance		
Life Insurance		
Medical not Covered		
Dental		
Cell Phone	50	600
Internet	50	600
TV		
Health Club	20	240
Clothing		
Christmas	1,000	1,000
Birthdays		
Entertainment		
Music/Movie/ect Subsciptions		
Vacation	2,500	2,500
Dining Out	100	1,200
School Supplies		
College Costs		
Other Hygene	30	360
Total Daily Living	$	$ 33,500

33,740

Household Budget
(page2)

Investment

Debt Reduction	$ ___	$ ___
Retirement Savings		
Collge Fund		
6-month Reserve		
Other		
Other		
Other		

Total Investment	$ ___	$ ___

Total	$ ___	$ ___

Business Budget
(page 1)

Broker	Monthly Cost	Annual Cost
Franchise Fee	$	$
Broker's Take on Each Sale		
E&O		
Annual Fee		
Transaction Fee		
Technology Fee		
Other Fee		
Other Fee		
Total Broker	$	$

Memberships	Monthly Cost	Annual Cost
MLS	$	$
Realtor Dues		
Designation Dues		
License		
Other		
Other		
Other		
Total Memberships	$	$

Marketing	Monthly Cost	Annual Cost
Internet Advertising	$	$
Print Ads		
Direct Mail		
Open Houses		
FSBO Program		
Expired Program		
Seminar Hosting		
Postage		
Printing		
CMA Software		
CRM Software		
Other		
Other		
Other		
Total Marketing	$	$

Business Budget
(page 2)

Operating Expenses

Closing Gifts	$ _____	$ _____
Office Supplies	_____	_____
Appt. Scheduling	_____	_____
Signs	_____	_____
Lockboxes	_____	_____
Business Cards	_____	_____
Coaching	_____	_____
Conventions	_____	_____
Education	_____	_____
Accountant	_____	_____
Assistant	_____	_____
Legal	_____	_____
Other	_____	_____
Other	_____	_____
Total Operating Expenses	_____	_____

Miscellaneous

Other	_____	_____
Other	_____	_____
Other	_____	_____
Other	_____	_____
Other	_____	_____
Other	_____	_____
Other	_____	_____
Total Miscellaneous	_____	_____

Total Business Expenses $ _____ $ _____

Desires

Cost

Home Improvements

    Landscaping   _____   _____

    Decoration   _____   _____

    Maintainance   _____   _____

    Other   _____   _____

    Other   _____   _____

    Other   _____   _____

Travel

_____   _____

_____   _____

_____   _____

_____   _____

_____   _____

Technology/Entertainment

_____   _____

_____   _____

_____   _____

Charity

_____   _____

_____   _____

_____   _____

Children/Grandchildren

_____   _____

_____   _____

Recreation

_____   _____

_____   _____

Other

_____   _____

_____   _____

_____   _____

_____   _____

_____   _____

Total   =========

73

Listing Activity Recap

	Client Name (or Address)	List/Sale Price	Outcome	Total Commission Paid	Source of Client
1					
2					
3					
4					
5					
6					
7					
8					
9					
10					
11					
12					
13					
14					
15					
16					
17					
18					
19					
20					
21					
22					
23					
24					
25					
26					
27					
28					

Summary

Total number of listings taken

Number of listings that sold

% of listings taken that sold

Average Sale Price $

Average Total Revenue/Listing $

Buyer Activity Recap

	Client Name (or Address)	List/Sale Price	Outcome	Total Commission Paid	Source of Client
1					
2					
3					
4					
5					
6					
7					
8					
9					
10					
11					
12					
13					
14					
15					
16					
17					
18					
19					
20					
21					
22					
23					
24					
25					
26					
27					
28					
29					
30					
31					
32					
33					
34					
35					
36					
37					

Other Revenue Recap

	Address	Type*	Total Commission $	Source of Client
1				
2				
3				
4				
5				
6				
7				
8				
9				
10				
11				
12				
13				
14				
15				
16				
17				
18				
19				
20				
21				
22				
23				
24				

* Rental, Referral, BPO, etc

Your Current Business

1 **How Many Listings Did You Take in the Last 12 Months?**   _____

2 **How Many of Those Listings Sold?**   _____
      (include those not yet sold but certain to sell)

3 **What % of Your Listings Sold?**   _____ %
      (Line 2/Line 1) x 100

4 **What Was the Average Commission % Paid for Listings?**   _____ %
      (the % you charge your sellers)

5 **What Was the Average Sale Price of Your Closed Listings?** $ _____

6 **What Was Your Average Total Commission/Listing Sold?** $ _____
      (Line 5 x Line 4)

7 **How Many Buyer Sides Did You Close?**   _____

8 **What Was the Average Commission % Paid For Buyer Sides?**   _____ %

9 **What Was Your Average Sale Price Per Buyer Side?** $ _____

10 **What Was Your Average Income/Sale For Your Buyer Sales?** $ _____
      (Line 8 x Line 9)

11 **How Many Total Sides Did You Close?**   _____

12 **How Many of Your Total Sides Closed Were Listings?**   _____
      (regardless of when the listing was taken)

13 **What % of Your Business Was Closed Listing Sides?**   _____ %
      (Line 12/Line 11) x 100

14 **What % of Your Business Was Closed Sales Sides?**   _____ %
      (Line 7/Line 11) x 100

Calculating Your Production Goals

1 **Income Needed From Your Real Estate Business?** $ _____
    (see 'The Grand Total')

2 **(Subtract) Estimated Total Income From Real Estate Activities**
    Other Than Listings and Sales (BPOs, rentals, etc.) - $ _____
    (use a conservative estimate based on your history)

3 **Total Income Needed From Listing and Selling -** $ _____

4 **Estimated Average Commission/Transaction Side -** $ _____
    (not your share, the total paid to your company)

5 **How Many Transaction Sides Must You Close ?**   _____
    (divide Line 3 by Line 4 - round up))

6 **What % Of Your Business Do You Want To Be From Listings?**   _____ %

7 **What % Of Your Business Do You Want To Be From Buyers?**   _____ %

8 **How Many Listings Must You Close?**   _____
    (multiply Line 5 by Line 6 - round up)

9 **How Many Buyer Sides Must You Close?**   _____
    (multiply Line 5 by Line 7 - round up)

10 **What % Of Your Listings Close?**   _____ %
    (use your recent history or make an educated estimate)

11 **How Many Listings Do You Need?**   _____
    (divide Line 8 by Line 10 - round up)

Your Target Numbers

Total Transactions Needed   _____

Total Listings Needed   _____

Total Closed Listings Needed   _____

Total Buyer Sides Needed   _____

The Grand Total

Budget Item	Cost
Household Expenses	_____
Business Expenses	_____
Desires	_____
Estimated Taxes	_____
The Grand Total	_____
Family income from other sources	_____
Income needed from real estate business	_____

Business Plan Summary

Goals   **Date:**

       Income   _____

       Listings Taken   _____

       Listings Sold   _____

       Buyer Sides   _____

       Total Sides   _____

Systems Which Will Be Used

1 _____

2 _____

3 _____

4 _____

5 _____

Source of Clients

System	Listings	Buyers
Total		

Methods of Staying 'On Track'

1 _____

2 _____

3 _____

4 _____

5 _____

_____

Professional Growth

_____

_____

_____

_____

_____

System Summary

System Title: _____

Objectives:

Listing Opportunities Created: _____

Buyer Opportunities Created: _____

Expected # of Closed Transaction Sides: _____

Expected Revenues: _____

Method

1 _____

2 _____

3 _____

4 _____

5 _____

6 _____

7 _____

8 _____

Schedule: _____

_____

_____

_____

_____

_____

_____

Expenses: _____

Profit: _____

System Summary

System Title: _____

Objectives:

Listing Opportunities Created: _____

Buyer Opportunities Created: _____

Expected # of Closed Transaction Sides: _____

Expected Revenues: _____

Method

1 _____

2 _____

3 _____

4 _____

5 _____

6 _____

7 _____

8 _____

Schedule: _____

_____

_____

_____

_____

_____

_____

Expenses: _____

Profit: _____

System Summary

System Title: _____

Objectives:

      Listing Opportunities Created: _____

      Buyer Opportunities Created: _____

      Expected # of Closed Transaction Sides: _____

      Expected Revenues: _____

Method

      1 _____

      2 _____

      3 _____

      4 _____

      5 _____

      6 _____

      7 _____

      8 _____

Schedule: _____

_____

_____

_____

_____

_____

_____

Expenses: _____

Profit: _____

System Summary

System Title: _____

Objectives:

Listing Opportunities Created: _____

Buyer Opportunities Created: _____

Expected # of Closed Transaction Sides: _____

Expected Revenues: _____

Method

1 _____

2 _____

3 _____

4 _____

5 _____

6 _____

7 _____

8 _____

Schedule: _____

_____

_____

_____

_____

_____

_____

Expenses: _____

Profit: _____

Appendix B

*Forms For
Measuring Progress*

Record of Closings

	Date	Listing /Sale?	Client	Sale Price	Commission	YTD Income	Source
1							
2							
3							
4							
5							
6							
7							
8							
9							
10							
11							
12							
13							
14							
15							
16							
17							
18							
19							
20							
21							
22							
23							
24							
25							
26							
27							
28							
29							
30							
31							
32							
33							
34							
35							
36							
37							
38							
39							

Open House System Summary

Date	Address	# of Visitors	# of Listing Leads	# of Buyer Leads	Successes

Direct Mail System Recap

Date	Mailing Piece	# Sent	Sent Where	Cost	Successes

FSBO Contact Recap

Date	Name	Address	Form of Contact?	Made Appt?	Outcome

Expired Listing Contact Recap

Date	Name	Address	Form of Contact?	Made Appt?	Outcome

Appendix C

Sample Business Plan

Business Plan Summary

Goals   **Date:**   9/20/17

Income	$179,084.00
Listings Taken	22
Listings Sold	16
Buyer Sides	7
Total Sides	23

Systems Which Will Be Used

1 Sphere of Influence
2 Direct Mail
3 Open House
4 Expired
5

Source of Clients

System	Listings	Buyers
SOI	6	3
Direct Mail	6	0
Open House	4	4
FSBO	0	0
Expired	6	0
Internet Ads		0
Total	22	7

Methods of Staying 'On Track'

1 Bi-weekly coaching phone call
2 Sunday night 30 minute review/plan time
3 Recap sheets for each system
4 Monthy breakfast with wife/partner to review business
5

Professional Growth

Redevelop pre-listing package
Attend NAR convention
Attend three motivational talks

Household Budget

Home	Monthly Cost	Annual Cost
Housing (Rent/Mortgage)	$1,754.00	$21,048.00
Property Taxes		$11,235.00
Heating Oil/Gas	$215.00	$2,580.00
Electric	$125.00	$1,500.00
Homwowners Insurance		$2,100.00
Lawn Service		$735.00
Snow Removal		$400.00
Home Improvements		$0.00
Water/Sewer	$35.00	$420.00
Other		$0.00
Other		$0.00
Total Home		$40,018.00

Daily Living	Monthly Cost	Annual Cost
Food	$600.00	$7,200.00
Car Payments	$435.00	$5,220.00
Car Maintainence		$2,000.00
Gasoline	$235.00	$2,820.00
Auto Insurance		$2,300.00
Health Insurance	$2,033.00	$24,396.00
Life Insurance	$350.00	$4,200.00
Medical not Covered		$9,750.00
Dental		$2,000.00
Cell Phone	$185.00	$2,220.00
Internet	$65.00	$780.00
TV	$35.00	$420.00
Health Club	$15.00	$180.00
Clothing		$1,500.00
Christmas		$3,000.00
Birthdays		$500.00
Entertainment	$200.00	$2,400.00
Music/Movie/ect Subsciptions	$40.00	$480.00
Vacation		$7,500.00
Dining Out	$200.00	$2,400.00
School Supplies		$400.00
College Costs		$0.00
Other		$0.00
Other		$0.00
Other		$0.00
Total Daily Living		$81,666.00

Household Budget

Investment

Debt Reduction		$4,000.00
Retirement Savings		$15,000.00
Collge Fund		$5,000.00
6-month Reserve		$0.00
Other		
Other		
Other		
Total Investment		$24,000.00

Total ⬜ $145,684.00

Business Budget

Broker

	Annual Cost
Franchise Fee (estimated)	$ 17,000.00
Broker's Take on Each Sale	57,500.00
E&O	750.00
Annual Fee	350.00
Transaction Fee	0.00
Technology Fee	250.00
Other Fee	0.00
Other Fee	0.00
Total Broker	$ 75,850.00

Memberships

MLS	$ 850.00
Realtor Dues	400.00
Designation Dues	1,250.00
License	50.00
Other	
Other	
Other	
Total Memberships	$ 2,550.00

Marketing

Internet Advertising	$ 3,600.00
Print Ads	1,200.00
Direct Mail	4,500.00
Open Houses	1,800.00
FSBO Program	1,200.00
Expired Program	1,900.00
Seminar Hosting	1,500.00
Postage	250.00
Printing	450.00
CMA Software	120.00
CRM Software	360.00
Website	3,000.00
Other	
Other	
Total Marketing	$ 19,880.00

Business Budget

Operating Expenses

Closing Gifts	$ 3,000.00
Office Supplies	900.00
Appt. Scheduling	450.00
Signs	400.00
Lockboxes	250.00
Business Cards	120.00
Coaching	4,000.00
Conventions	2,000.00
Education	1,000.00
Accountant	1,200.00
Assistant	0.00
Legal	0.00
Other	
Other	

Total Operating Expenses	13,320.00

Miscellaneous

	0.00
Other	0.00
Other	0.00
Other	0.00
Other	0.00
Other	0.00
Other	0.00
Other	0.00
Other	0.00

Total Miscellaneous	0.00

Total Business Expenses	$ 111,600.00

119

Desires

			Cost
Home Improvements			
	Landscaping	Patio & Firepit	$6,000.00
	Decoration	New carpet	$1,500.00
	Maintainance	Seal driveway	$400.00
	Other		
	Other		
	Other		
Travel			
	Cruise w/family		$8,000.00
	2, 5-day 'get-a-ways'		$3,500.00
Technology/Entertainment			
	iPad Pro		$700.00
	New phone		$700.00
Charity			
	Mission trip to DR		$2,000.00
Children/Grandchildren			
	Grandkids college fund		$1,000.00
Recreation			
	Golf		$3,000.00
Other			
Total			$26,800.00

Listing Activity Recap

	Client Name (or Address)	List/Sale Price	Outcome	Total Commission Paid	Source of Client
1	6 Roxanne	$250,000	Expired	$0.00	DM - JS Card
2	1968 Clove	$425,000	Sold	$10,625.00	Sphere of influence
3	30 Meadowood	$475,000	Sold	$11,875.00	Sphere of influence
4	48 Fulton	$269,900	Withdrawn	$0.00	Open house
5	12 Country	$425,000	Sold	$10,625.00	Sphere of influence
6	141 Widmer	$459,850	Foreclosed on	$0.00	Sphere of influence
7	4 Gentry	$650,000	Expired	$0.00	DM - JS Card
8	275 Cream	$320,000	Sold	$8,000.00	Sphere of influence
9	15 Innsbruck	$385,000	Sold	$9,625.00	Open house
10	27 Sherwood	$299,000	Sold	$7,475.00	DM - out of area
11	1 Buttonwood	$239,000	Sold	$5,975.00	DM - out of area
12	10 Cady	$275,000	Sold	$6,875.00	Sphere of influence
13	669 S Hillside	$225,000	Sold	$5,625.00	Open house
14	159 Wilkes	$200,000	Sold	$5,000.00	Expired
15	35 Crescent	$245,000	Sold	$6,125.00	Expired
16	9 Oakwood	$175,000	Sold	$4,375.00	Sphere of influence
17					
18	Total	$5,317,750		$92,200.00	
19					
20					
21					
22	Sphere of Influence	7			
23	Direct Mail	4			
24	Open House	3			
25	Expired	2			
26					
27					
28					

Summary

Total number of listings taken		16
Number of listings that sold		12
% of listings taken that sold		75
Average List Price	$	$332,359.38
Average Total Revenue/Listing	$	$7,683.33

Buyer Activity Recap

	Client Name (or Address)	Sale Price	Outcome	Total Commission Paid	Source of Client
1	Johnson	$0	Bought w/other agent		Sphere of influence
2	Reed	$265,000	Sale	$6,625.00	Sign call
3	Booth	$315,000	Sale	$7,875.00	Open house - Rusk
4	Culkin	$0	Did not buy anything	$0.00	Sphere of influence
5	Amerse	$0	Unknown	$0.00	Zillow
6	Rice	$176,000	Sale	$4,400.00	Sphere of influence
7	Wells	$425,000	Sale	$10,625.00	Open house - Reed
8	Wickman	$0	Bought w/other agent	$0.00	Sign call
9	Amato	$0	Still looking	$0.00	Sphere of influence
10	Nunez	$0	Unknown - no reply	$0.00	Open house - Reed
11	Best	$0	Still looking	$0.00	Sphere of influence
12	Rodriquez	$345,000	Sale	$8,625.00	Zillow
13	Haggarty	$0	Lost job	$0.00	Open house - Reed
14	Quinn	$0	Bought w/other agent	$0.00	Zillow
15	Pearson	$0	Bought FSBO	$0.00	Open house - Rusk
16	Archer	$287,000	Sale	$7,175.00	Sphere of influence
17	Cunningham	$0	Did not buy anything	$0.00	Sign call
18	Babcock	$195,000	Sale	$4,875.00	Open house - Alves
19					
20	Total			$50,200.00	
21					
22					
23	Sphere of influence	6			
24	Sign call	3			
25	Open houses	6			
26	Zillow	3			
27	Total	18			
28					
29					
30					
31					
32					
33					
34					
35					
36					
37					

Your Current Business

1	How Many Listings Did You Take in the Last 12 Months?	16
2	How Many of Those Listings Sold? (include those not yet sold but certain to sell)	12
3	What % of Your Listings Sold? (Line 2/Line 1) x 100	75%
4	What Was the Average Commission % Paid for Listings? (the % you charge your sellers)	2.50%
5	What Was the Average Sale Price of Your Closed Listings?	$307,333
6	What Was Your Average Total Commission/Listing Sold? (Line 5 x Line 4)	$7,683.33
7	How Many Buyer Sides Did You Close?	7
8	What Was the Average Commission % Paid For Buyer Sides?	2.50%
9	What Was Your Average Sale Price Per Buyer Side?	$286,857
10	What Was Your Average Income/Sale For Your Buyer Sales? (Line 8 x Line 9)	$7,171.43
11	How Many Total Sides Did You Close?	19
12	How Many of Your Total Sides Closed Were Listings? (regardless of when the listing was taken)	12
13	What % of Your Business Was Closed Listing Sides? (Line 12/Line 11) x 100	63.16%
14	What % of Your Business Was Closed Sales Sides? (Line 7/Line 11) x 100	36.84%

Calculating Your Production Goals

1 **Income Needed From Your Real Estate Business?**	$179,084.00
(see page 26 - 'The Grand Total')	
2 **(Subtract) Estimated Total Income From Real Estate Activities**	
Other Than Listings and Sales (BPOs, rentals, etc.) -	$5,000.00
(use a conservative estimate based on your history)	
3 **Total Income Needed From Listing and Selling -**	$174,084.00
4 **Estimated Average Commission/Transaction Side -**	$7,500.00
(not your share, the total paid to your company)	
5 **How Many Transaction Sides Must You Close ?**	23.2
(divide Line 3 by Line 4 - round up))	
6 **What % Of Your Business Do You Want To Be From Listings?**	70.00%
7 **What % Of Your Business Do You Want To Be From Buyers?**	30.00%
8 **How Many Listings Must You Close?**	16.2
(multiply Line 5 by Line 6 - round up)	
9 **How Many Buyer Sides Must You Close?**	7.0
(multiply Line 5 by Line 7 - round up)	
10 **What % Of Your Listings Close?**	75.00%
(use your recent history or make an educated estimate)	
11 **How Many Listings Do You Need?**	21.66
(divide Line 8 by Line 10 - round up)	

Your Target Numbers

Total Transactions Needed	23
Total Listings Needed	22
Total Closed Listings Needed	16
Total Buyer Sides Needed	7

The Grand Total

Budget Item	Cost
Household Expenses	$145,684.00
Business Expenses	$111,600.00
Desires	$26,800.00
Estimated Taxes	$30,000.00
The Grand Total	**$314,084.00**
Family income from other sources	$135,000.00
Income needed from real estate business	**$179,084.00**

System Summary

System Title: Sphere of Influence

Objectives:

Listing Opportunities Created:	6
Buyer Opportunities Created:	3
Expected # of Closed Transaction Sides:	8
Expected Revenues:	$60,000.00

Method

1 Mail poscard or letter to SOI 12x/year

2 Email flyer of new listing 12x/year

3 Call two people on my list of 200 names each day

4 Host a 'client appreciation' event in October

5 _____

6 _____

7 _____

8 _____

Schedule: Just Sold pcs sent on the 2nd Wed of ech month except Feb & Dec

Send Calendar in December

Send 'growing my business' letter in March

Useful real estate postings 2x/week on Facebook

Apple pie giveaway at Client Appreciation event in November

Email with new listing 4th Thur of each month

Expenses: $2,200.00

Profit: $57,800.00

System Summary

System Title: Direct Mail

Objectives:

Listing Opportunities Created:	6
Buyer Opportunities Created:	0
Expected # of Closed Transaction Sides:	5
Expected Revenues:	$38,000.00

Method

1 400 Just Sold cards EDDM - every sale

2 10 'Out of area' letters/week

3 10 'longtime owner' letter/week

4 _____

5 _____

6 _____

7 _____

8 _____

Schedule: Just Sold cards sent the day of closing

Out of area letters sent on Wednesday

Longtime owners letter sent on Wednesday

_____

_____

_____

_____

Expenses: $3,500.00

Profit: $34,500.00

Direct Mail System Recap

Date	Mailing Piece	# Sent	Sent Where	Cost	Successes

System Summary

System Title: Open House

Objectives:

Listing Opportunities Created:	4
Buyer Opportunities Created:	4
Expected # of Closed Transaction Sides:	7
Expected Revenues:	$52,500.00

Method

1 Host 17 'Perfect' Open Houses

2 Select attractive, well-located homes

3 Invite neighbors

4 Follow the 'Perfect Open House checklist' (see attached)

5

6

7

8

Schedule: 2 each in Feb, May, Oct

3 each in Mar, Apr, Sept

1 in Jan & Jun

0 in Dec, Jul, Aug, Nov

Expenses: $1,800.00

Profit: $50,700.00

The Perfect Open House Checklist

Two Weeks Before:

Select the host house
      The right area? The best price range? The right location?

Confirm with the homeowner the open house and they will not be there on Sunday

The Week Before:

Let Liz know so she can place the ad - Monday

Place 'Open House' rider on sign - Monday

Mail invitations to neighbors - Tuesday

If not your listing – visit the home and complete 76 Questions – No later than Tuesday

Prepare Executive Edge flyer for printing and email – Tuesday

Email flyer to your 'book of business' as well as real estate community – Wednesday

Update your Facebook page, conversationally inviting friends to come - Wednesday

Identify two 'crossover properties' for discussion - Friday

Print out 10 flyers on high quality paper - Friday

Print out 10 MLS listing sheets - Friday

Print out 10 personal brochures - Friday

Print 'Sign In' sheets (2) - Friday

Prepare Lucite brochure stand with flyer - Friday

Prepare snacks, drinks for neighbors – Saturday
      (Pepperidge Farm cookies, bottled water, ice tea)

The Day Of:

Place directional signs with balloons – reserve some balloons for kids

Arrive at open house 30 minutes early – inspect house thoroughly

Set out sign-in sheets, snacks, Lucite brochure stand, welcome mat, etc

Add sign-in names to your database.

Call visitors (when possible) to thank and ask feedback

Add names to database and assign to groups (open house, specific house, buyers)

Send Toolkit CMA to each visitor with email address

Within One Week:

Call to visitors with news of other listings

Email messages

Message to real estate community:

Subject: Open House – Send Your Buyers!

Hi (contact first name)!

I am hosting an open house this Sunday, June 27 from 1-4 PM. I thought you might have a buyer and I wanted to encourage you to send them. Don't worry about having to accompany them – I will honor your relationship with them.

Best wishes,

Message to your book of business:

Subject: I Am Hosting An Open House And YOU Are Invited!

Hi (contact first name)!

I wanted to let you know I am hosting an open house this Sunday and I would love it if you stopped in to say 'Hi'. It's easy to find – just off Route 44.

Hope to see you Sunday!

Best wishes,

Open House kit:

Supply of –

Purchase offers	Pens – not giveaways
Calculator	Personal brochures
Business cards	Mortgage calculation chart
Pad of paper	CD of relaxing music
WD-40	Air freshener
Dust rag and Pledge	Toilet paper
Mouthwash	Eye drops
Weekly Planning sheets	

A Word on Dress:

You should always view an open house as a job interview – because it is. You should dress to impress. You can NEVER go wrong wearing slacks, solid color shirt, and a tie. Be sure your shoes are shined.

Never wear jeans, shorts, t-shirt, sandals or athletic shoes.

Dress as you would for a really important listing presentation.

Open House Recap

Date: _____   Weather:

Address: _____

Price: _____

Advertised where?   _____
                         _____
                         _____

# of Letters to neighbors: _____

# of Visitors: _____
# of Buyer Prospects: _____
# of Listing Prospects: _____

Follow up items: _____
         _____
         _____
         _____
         _____
         _____

Comments: _____
          _____

Open House System Summary

Date	Address	# of Visitors	# of Listing Leads	# of Buyer Leads	Successes

System Summary

System Title: Expired

Objectives:

Listing Opportunities Created:	6
Buyer Opportunities Created:	0
Expected # of Closed Transaction Sides:	4
Expected Revenues:	$30,000.00

Method

1 Identify old expireds - min 6 months prior

2 Send 'old expired' letter

3 Follow up with phone call

4

5

6

7

8

Schedule: Each week mail to 10 old expireds

Each week call 10 expireds

Expenses: $500.00

Profit: $29,500.00

Expired Listing Contact Recap

Date	Name	Address	Form of Contact?	Made Appt?	Outcome

Record of Closings

	Date	Listing /Sale?	Client	Sale Price	Commission	YTD Income	Source
1							
2							
3							
4							
5							
6							
7							
8							
9							
10							
11							
12							
13							
14							
15							
16							
17							
18							
19							
20							
21							
22							
23							
24							
25							
26							
27							
28							
29							
30							
31							
32							
33							
34							
35							
36							
37							
38							
39							

About the Author

Matt Williams is the broker and owner of Realty Executives – Williams-Sykes Realty located in Dutchess County New York. He has written articles for Realtor Magazine, Supervisor, 100% Magazine, and The Residential Specialist. He is the author of *Planning For Success in Real Estate Sales – Your Guide To Creating A Winning Business Plan* and *Never Try To Negotiate With A Drunken Homeowner . . . and 800 Other Things Every Real Estate Agent Should Know.*

All proceeds from this book will be donated to the
Michael J. Fox Foundation For Parkinson's Research

Commit to the Lord whatever you do and your plans will succeed.
- Proverbs 16:3 (NIV)

CPSIA information can be obtained
at www.ICGtesting.com
Printed in the USA
BVHW01s1802010718
520553BV00015B/207/P

9 781976 095184